DATE DUE

STATES

MINNESOTA

A MyReportLinks.com Book

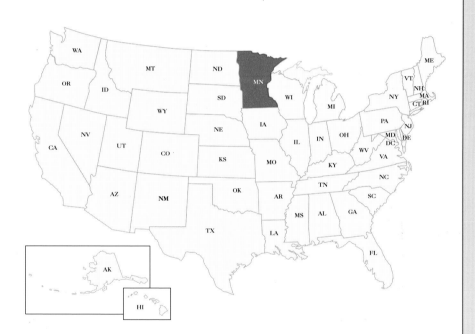

Stephen Feinstein

MyReportLinks.com Books

an imprint of

 Enslow Publishers, Inc.

Box 398, 40 Industrial Road
Berkeley Heights, NJ 07922
USA

MyReportLinks.com Books, an imprint of Enslow Publishers, Inc. MyReportLinks is a trademark of Enslow Publishers, Inc.

Library of Congress Cataloging-in-Publication Data

Feinstein, Stephen.
  Minnesota / Stephen Feinstein.
    p. cm. — (States)
Summary: Discusses the land and climate, economy, government, and history of the North Star State. Includes Internet links to Web sites related to Minnesota.
Includes bibliographical references and index.
  ISBN 0-7660-5096-3
  1. Minnesota—Juvenile literature. [1. Minnesota.] I. Title. II. Series: States (Series : Berkeley Heights, N.J.)
F606.3.F45 2003
977.6—dc21

                          2002014850

Printed in the United States of America

10 9 8 7 6 5 4 3 2 1

To Our Readers:
Through the purchase of this book, you and your library gain access to the Report Links that specifically back up this book.
The Publisher will provide access to the Report Links that back up this book and will keep these Report Links up to date on **www.myreportlinks.com** for three years from the book's first publication date.
We have done our best to make sure all Internet addresses in this book were active and appropriate when we went to press. However, the author and the Publisher have no control over, and assume no liability for, the material available on those Internet sites or on other Web sites they may link to.
The usage of the MyReportLinks.com Books Web site is subject to the terms and conditions stated on the Usage Policy Statement on **www.myreportlinks.com**.
In the future, a password may be required to access the Report Links that back up this book. The password is found on the bottom of page 4 of this book.
Any comments or suggestions can be sent by e-mail to comments@myreportlinks.com or to the address on the back cover.

Photo Credits: America's Story from America's Library/Library of Congress, p. 28; © Corel, pp. 3, 17, 19, 21, 41; © 1995 Photodisc, pp. 30, 43; © 1999 Photodisc, pp. 31, 45; © 2001 Robesus, Inc., p. 10 (flag); City of Brooklyn Park, Minnesota, p. 25; Enslow Publisher, Inc, pp. 1, 20; Eyewire Cities of America, p. 11; LBJ Library Photo by Yoichi R. Okamoto, p. 33; Library of Congress, pp. 3 (Constitution), 35; Minnesota Historical Society, pp. 15, 26, 37; Minnesota Office of Tourism, pp. 13, 22; Minnesota State University, p. 39; MyReportLinks.com Books, p. 4.

Cover Photo: © 1995, PhotoDisc, Inc.

Cover Description: Downtown Minneapolis.

Tools

Search

Notes
Discuss
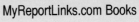
MyReportLinks.com Books

Go!

Contents

MyReportLinks.com Books
Great Books, Great Links, Great for Research!

MyReportLinks.com Books present the information you need to learn about your report subject. In addition, they show you where to go on the Internet for more information. The pre-evaluated Report Links that back up this book are kept up to date on **www.myreportlinks.com**. With the purchase of a MyReportLinks.com Books title, you and your library gain access to the Report Links that specifically back up that book. The Report Links save hours of research time and link to dozens—even hundreds—of Web sites, source documents, and photos related to your report topic.

Please see "To Our Readers" on the Copyright page for important information about this book, the MyReportLinks.com Books Web site, and the Report Links that back up this book.

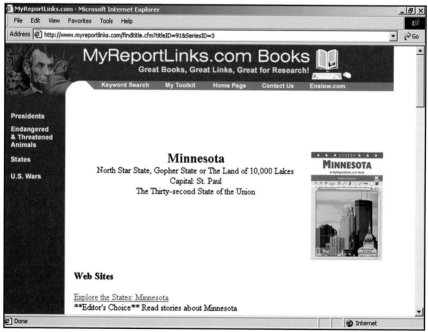

Access:

The Publisher will provide access to the Report Links that back up this book and will try to keep these Report Links up to date on our Web site for three years from the book's first publication date. Please enter **SMN2198** if asked for a password.

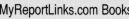
Report Links

The Internet sites described below can be accessed at
http://www.myreportlinks.com

*EDITOR'S CHOICE

▶ **Explore the States: Minnesota**
America's Story from America's Library, a Library of Congress Web site,
provides a brief description of Minnesota. You will also find links to
interesting stories about Minnesota and learn why Minnesota is
considered the Halloween capital.

Link to this Internet site from http://www.myreportlinks.com

*EDITOR'S CHOICE

▶ **Minnesota Historical Society**
The Minnesota Historical Society's Web site provides information
about the state's historic places as well as the museum's holdings.

Link to this Internet site from http://www.myreportlinks.com

*EDITOR'S CHOICE

▶ *World Almanac for Kids Online:* **Minnesota**
The *World Almanac for Kids Online* provides facts and statistics about
Minnesota. The state economy, history, its land and resources, and
population are among the topics covered.

Link to this Internet site from http://www.myreportlinks.com

*EDITOR'S CHOICE

▶ **U.S. Census Bureau: Minnesota**
At the U.S. Census Bureau Web site you will find quick facts relating
to the 2000 census, including information about Minnesota's people,
businesses, and geography.

Link to this Internet site from http://www.myreportlinks.com

*EDITOR'S CHOICE

▶ **Today In History: Minnesota**
"Today in History" tells the story of the day that Minnesota was
admitted into the Union. Here you will learn about the controversy
that postponed the acceptance of Minnesota's application for statehood.

Link to this Internet site from http://www.myreportlinks.com

*EDITOR'S CHOICE

▶ **History of Minnesota**
The History of Minnesota Web site provides a time line of the state's
history from 1659 to 1998. You will also learn about immigration to
Minnesota and find out about state facts and symbols.

Link to this Internet site from http://www.myreportlinks.com

Report Links

The Internet sites described below can be accessed at
http://www.myreportlinks.com

▶ All About Minnesota

This site, administered by the Minnesota Office of Tourism and the Minnesota Historical Society, provides information about Minnesota's state symbols, economy, history, and statistics.

Link to this Internet site from http://www.myreportlinks.com

▶ Ancestral Trails

The Ancestral Trails Web site provides historical information about the first people of Minnesota.

Link to this Internet site from http://www.myreportlinks.com

▶ Bob Dylan

Bob Dylan, a native of Minnesota, was voted one of *Time* magazine's most influential people of the century in the category of artists and entertainers. At this Web site you will find a brief profile of his life and musical career.

Link to this Internet site from http://www.myreportlinks.com

▶ Death of the Dream

This PBS documentary explores farmhouses in the "Heartland of America." Learn about the people who settled in these areas, the land, and how modern technology led to the destruction of many of these homes. You can also take a virtual tour of a farmhouse.

Link to this Internet site from http://www.myreportlinks.com

▶ Demographic Profile of Minnesota

The University of Minnesota provides access to the United States census report for the year 2000. At this Web site you can scroll through data sets and read articles related to the census reports.

Link to this Internet site from http://www.myreportlinks.com

▶ Eidem Homestead Brooklyn Park Historical Farm

The Eidem Homestead Brooklyn Park Historical Farm Web site provides a history of what farm life was like in Minnesota from the year 1890 to 1910. Here you can learn about the Eidem family and view images of the farm.

Link to this Internet site from http://www.myreportlinks.com

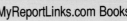
Report Links

 The Internet sites described below can be accessed at
http://www.myreportlinks.com

▶ **Explore Minnesota**
This site is packed with information about travel and vacation
destinations across Minnesota. You will also find travel stories
and maps.

Link to this Internet site from http://www.myreportlinks.com

▶ **F. Scott Fitzgerald Centenary Homepage**
This Web site provides access to many resources about native
Minnesotan F. Scott Fitzgerald. Here you will find a brief biography,
essays, articles, and facts about the writer, as well as writings by
Fitzgerald, himself.

Link to this Internet site from http://www.myreportlinks.com

▶ **Governor "The Mind" Ventura**
PBS provides a brief overview of the current governor of Minnesota,
Jesse Ventura. Here you will learn about his views on education,
the environment, and his relationship with the press.

Link to this Internet site from http://www.myreportlinks.com

▶ **Hennepin History Museum**
At the Hennepin History Museum in Minneapolis, Minnesota, you can
explore the museum's many online exhibits, including *Documenting the
Ordinary: The Suburban Documentation Project.*

Link to this Internet site from http://www.myreportlinks.com

▶ **Hmong Cultural Center Inc.**
At the Hmong Cultural Center Inc. Web site you can learn about the
Hmong people. According to the United States census, Minnesota has
the second-largest population of Hmong in the country.

Link to this Internet site from http://www.myreportlinks.com

▶ **Laura Ingalls Wilder Was Born February 7, 1867**
America's Story from America's Library, a Library of Congress Web site,
tells the life story of Laura Ingalls Wilder, who spent much of her
childhood in Minnesota.

Link to this Internet site from http://www.myreportlinks.com

Report Links

The Internet sites described below can be accessed at
http://www.myreportlinks.com

▶ **Mall of America**

The largest indoor mall in the United States is located in Minneapolis, Minnesota. This official Web site presents an introduction to and information about the Mall of America.

Link to this Internet site from http://www.myreportlinks.com

▶ **Minnesota Author Biographies Project**

The Minnesota Author Biographies Project provides biographical sketches of thirty-six Minnesotan authors, including Laura Ingalls Wilder, F. Scott Fitzgerald, and many others.

Link to this Internet site from http://www.myreportlinks.com

▶ **Minnesota Data and Maps**

Minnesota Planning provides a variety of data sets and maps. Here you will find statistics on demographics, crime, and much more.

Link to this Internet site from http://www.myreportlinks.com

▶ **Minnesota DNR**

The state's Department of Natural Resources Web site provides a portal to Minnesota's seventy-two state parks. Also included is extensive information about the state's wildlife, history, geology, and landscape.

Link to this Internet site from http://www.myreportlinks.com

▶ **Minnesota Lake Finder**

Minnesota counts more than ten thousand lakes among its natural treasures. This site provides a guide to many of them. Click on "Recreation Compass" to view the interactive mapping tool.

Link to this Internet site from http://www.myreportlinks.com

▶ **Minnesota Place Names**

The Minnesota Place Names Web site tells the story behind the names of places, people, lakes, and streams in Minnesota.

Link to this Internet site from http://www.myreportlinks.com

Report Links

▼ The Internet sites described below can be accessed at
http://www.myreportlinks.com

▶ **Minnesota State Constitution**

At this Web site you will find the full text of the Minnesota
State Constitution.

Link to this Internet site from http://www.myreportlinks.com

▶ **Minnesota State Legislature**

The Minnesota State Legislature Web site includes information on the
state's house of representatives, senate, and laws. You will also find
"Youth Pages" with information just for kids.

Link to this Internet site from http://www.myreportlinks.com

▶ **North Star**

The North Star Web site provides access to information about
government offices, directories, and online services. You will also find a
kids section with key information about Minnesota.

Link to this Internet site from http://www.myreportlinks.com

▶ **Pioneering the Upper Midwest**

Explore the history of the upper Midwest through the Library of
Congress' special presentation, "Pioneering the Upper Midwest." Here
you will find images and learn about the land, its inhabitants, and how
the upper Midwest has evolved over the years.

Link to this Internet site from http://www.myreportlinks.com

▶ **Visual Resources Database**

The Visual Resource Database Web site holds 250,000 images,
including photographs, posters, and art relating to Minnesota's history.

Link to this Internet site from http://www.myreportlinks.com

▶ **Walnut Grove, Minnesota**

At this Web site you can explore the home of Laura Ingalls Wilder.
View pictures of the land, and read a brief biography about her life and
the history of Walnut Grove.

Link to this Internet site from http://www.myreportlinks.com

Minnesota Facts

Capital
Saint Paul

Gained Statehood
May 11, 1858, the thirty-second state.

Population
4,919,479*

Counties
87

Bird
Common loon

Tree
Norway pine (red pine)

Flower
Pink and white lady slipper

Fish
Walleye or walleyed pike

Mushroom
Morel

Gemstone
Lake Superior agate

Song
"Hail! Minnesota" (words by Truman E. Rickard and Arthur E. Upson, music by Truman E. Rickard)

Motto
"L'Étoile du Nord" (from the French "star of the north")

Population reflects the 2000 census.

Nicknames
Gopher State, North Star State, Land of 10,000 Lakes, Land of Sky-Blue Waters, Bread and Butter State

Seal
The official state seal shows three symbols: an American Indian on horseback, which recalls the state's American Indian heritage; a tree stump, which highlights the state's lumber industry; and a farmer plowing near the Falls of St. Anthony, which represents Minnesota's agriculture. The state motto—"L'Étoile du Nord"—also appears on the seal.

Flag
The seal appears in a circle, ringed by a wreath of lady slippers, on a royal-blue background edged in gold fringe. Circling the wreath is a ring of nineteen gold stars. One star is larger than the others. It represents Minnesota, the nineteenth state to join the union after the original thirteen states did.

The State of Minnesota

The Dakota word *minisota* means "sky-tinted waters." The Dakota Indians gave this poetic name to the river we now know as the Minnesota River. The state was named after the river.[1] Scattered throughout Minnesota are more than fifteen thousand lakes. Most of these, some quite large, are in the north woods. This is the land of the *voyageurs*, or "travelers." The name fit the French fur traders of the sixteenth and seventeenth centuries. These explorers of Minnesota's waterways were true voyageurs.

▲ Minnesota is home to major cities as well as rich farmland and forests. Pictured here is Minneapolis, the state's largest city, overlooking the Mississippi River.

Much of northern Minnesota is still covered by thick pine forests and lakes. Here the cry of the loon is often heard.

Some of Minnesota's "sky-tinted waters" are in the central and southern parts of the state. These regions are very different from northern Minnesota. It is a land of rolling farmlands with rich, fertile soil. Minnesota's largest cities, Minneapolis and St. Paul (the Twin Cities), are located there. Duluth, the state's third-largest city, is located in the north on the southwestern shore of Lake Superior.

▶ "Land of Blond Hair and Blue Ears"

Minnesotans with a sense of humor sometimes refer to their state as the "land of blond hair and blue ears."[2] Of course, they are referring to their state's cold, snowy winters. In addition, many Minnesotans are of northern-European descent, made obvious by their blond hair and blue eyes. More than 90 percent of the state's nearly 5 million people are descendants of immigrants from Norway, Sweden, Finland, Denmark, Germany, Austria, Russia, Poland, Ireland, and Britain. About 3 percent of the population is African American, and 3 percent is Hispanic American. Among the 3 percent of Asian-American Minnesotans are about twenty thousand Hmong from the country of Laos. The state's fifty thousand American Indians are mainly Chippewa (called the Ojibwe in Canada) and Dakota.[3]

▶ Lovers of the Outdoors

Minnesotans have a great love of the outdoors. Winter weather can be frigid. On occasion, the temperature will remain well below zero for days at a time. Hardy Minnesotans and visitors seem to find it energizing. In their leisure time, many flock to the woods to go

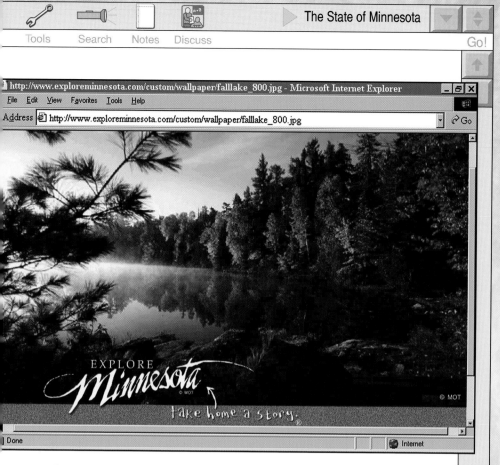

http://www.exploreminnesota.com/custom/wallpaper/falllake_800.jpg - Microsoft Internet Explorer

File   Edit   View   Favorites   Tools   Help

Address   http://www.exploreminnesota.com/custom/wallpaper/falllake_800.jpg   Go

EXPLORE
Minnesota
© MOT

take home a story.®

© MOT

Done   Internet

▲ *It is not surprising that people travel from out of state to experience the great outdoors of Minnesota.*

cross-country skiing. Others go ice fishing. They bore holes in the ice on frozen lakes and sit there patiently waiting to catch a fish. Back in town, winter festivals draw huge crowds. The St. Paul Winter Carnival features ice-skating races and ice-sculpture contests.

In the summer, Minnesotans and out-of-state visitors can experience the north woods as modern-day voyageurs. At Voyageurs National Park and Grand Portage National Monument, vacationers go canoeing through the forest. Often it is necessary to carry, or "portage," the canoe and gear from one lake to the next. The Boundary Waters

Canoe Area Wilderness in the Superior National Forest is quite different from other parks in the state. It is reserved only for travel by canoe. There are no roads in the area.

When the Going Gets Tough, the Tough Go Shopping

Minnesotans in Minneapolis can go shopping in a glassed-in Minneapolis-in-the-air. There they can shop to their heart's content protected from the cold outside. This city within a city is a maze of artificial streets and plazas. It is set in midair, four stories above the ground. Glassed-in skyways lead from block to block.

Only people who love to shop can truly appreciate the Mall of America. Opened in 1992, the mall is located in Bloomington, a suburb of the Twin Cities. The Mall of America is the largest shopping center in the nation. It is the second largest in the world; the West Edmonton Mall in Alberta, Canada, is the largest. The Mall of America contains more than five hundred stores. There are also many restaurants, a bank, a clinic, movie theaters, and a business school. In addition, there is an amusement park with a roller coaster, a wedding chapel, and still other attractions. The mall draws about 42.5 million customers per year. Enclosed beneath one enormous roof, it is as tall as an eight-story building. The mall structure takes up 45 acres and continues to grow.

Inspired by the North Country

Musician and poet Bob Dylan (birth name Robert Allen Zimmerman) was born in Duluth in 1941. In 1961, Dylan moved away from his native Minnesota to seek fame and fortune in New York City. The lyrics of the folk songs he wrote often dealt with important issues of the day.

"Blowin' in the Wind" is a good example. Dylan captured the essence of the northern Minnesota border country in his song "Girl from the North Country." His words "Where the wind hits heavy on the borderline" describe well what awaits travelers to the region.

Another famous Minnesota musician chose to remain in Minnesota. Prince Rogers Nelson was born in Minneapolis in 1958. He achieved remarkable success in the world of rock music with his band called The Revolution. Their album *Purple Rain* is one of the best-selling albums in music history. Eventually he started his own record label, Paisley Park, in the Twin Cities, which lasted until 1994.

▲ *F. Scott Fitzgerald was born in St. Paul, Minnesota. While living there, he finished his first successful novel,* This Side of Paradise.

Storyteller Garrison Keillor was born in Anoka, Minnesota, in 1942. His keen reflections of life in Minnesota gave birth to his unique brand of humor. Millions of people around the country listen to his weekly radio show, *A Prairie Home Companion.* The show consists of humorous stories about Lake Wobegon. In this fictional Minnesota town, all of the women are strong, men are good looking, and children are above average.

Several well-known American writers were born in Minnesota. Sinclair Lewis (1885–1951) probably based his novel *Main Street* (published in 1920) on his hometown of Sauk Centre. F. Scott Fitzgerald (1896–1940), born in St. Paul, is best known for his novel *The Great Gatsby* (1925). Minnesota is also home to journalist and author Harrison Salisbury and poet Robert Bly.

Charles A. Lindbergh (1902–74) spent his boyhood along the Mississippi River in the town of Little Falls, Minnesota. His flight across the Atlantic in 1927 sparked a revolution in aviation. Today, at Charles A. Lindbergh State Park, visitors can tour his home and see hundreds of photos and artifacts. There is also a full-scale replica of the *Spirit of St. Louis* cockpit. Visitors can step inside to envision flying across the Atlantic Ocean.[4]

Land and Climate

Minnesota is the nation's twelfth-largest state and the largest in the Midwest. It covers an area of about eighty-four thousand square miles. It is bordered on the north by the Canadian provinces of Manitoba and Ontario. Lake Superior and the state of Wisconsin form the state's eastern border. Iowa is to the south. South Dakota and North Dakota form Minnesota's western boundary.

▲ The Lake of the Woods borders Minnesota and Canada in the northwestern part of the state. It is just one of many reasons why the state is nicknamed the Land of 10,000 Lakes and the Land of Sky-Blue Waters.

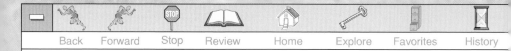

Nicknames and Geography

Three of Minnesota's nicknames refer to aspects of the state's geography. Minnesota is called the North Star State because of the state's Northwest Angle. This small area juts north across a portion of the Lake of the Woods on Minnesota's northern border. The Northwest Angle is the most northern point in the United States except for Alaska. "Land of Sky-Blue Waters" and "Land of 10,000 Lakes" are two other Minnesota nicknames. Both refer to the thousands of lakes scattered across the state.

Too Many Lakes to Count

Nobody knows for sure how many lakes there are in Minnesota. It all depends on how large a body of water has to be before it is considered as a lake. In Minnesota, opinions vary as to when a pond becomes a lake. Ten thousand sounds like too many lakes to fit inside one state. However, most geographers estimate that Minnesota has more than fifteen thousand. Of these, 11,842 are larger than ten acres. According to some people, Minnesota has as many as twenty-two thousand lakes!

So where did all these lakes come from? During the Ice Age, a series of thick glaciers covered most of Minnesota. The massive piles of ice flattened the land beneath. They left behind gently-rolling plains in most places. The glaciers began melting about 2 million years ago, resulting in their retreat across Minnesota. The last of the glaciers began to retreat less than twenty thousand years ago. When the ice completely melted, the low places filled with water. In a sense, Minnesota's lakes were a gift of the retreating glaciers. These lakes cover more than 4,750 square miles.

The largest lake entirely within the borders of Minnesota is Red Lake. It covers 430 square miles in the northern part of the state. Lake of the Woods is even larger, but part of it is in Canada. Other large Minnesota lakes include Rainy Lake, also on the Canadian border, and Mille Lacs Lake, Leech Lake, and Lake Winnibigoshish. Lake Itasca in northern Minnesota is the source of the Mississippi River. It is the nation's longest river. Other major Minnesota rivers include the St. Croix River, the Red River of the North, the Minnesota River, the St. Louis River, and the Crow River.

There are two legends about Lake Itasca. One involves Babe, the giant blue ox who was a companion of the legendary lumberjack Paul Bunyan. It is said that Babe created Lake Itasca and the Mississippi River by accidentally tipping over a water tank in a logging camp. Paul Bunyan did something even more amazing. According to legend, he scooped out the Great Lakes

▲ *Many can hear the cry of the common loon, Minnesota's state bird, in the state's northern forests and lakes.*

when Babe was thirsty and needed water bowls. Today enormous statues of Paul Bunyan and Babe stand on the shore of Lake Bemidji, in Bemidji, Minnesota.

The other Lake Itasca legend belongs to the Chippewa Indians. According to the Chippewa, the lake was named after I-tesk-a, the daughter of Hiawatha. Attracted by her great beauty, the lord of the underworld carried her away. I-tesk-a wept, and her tears formed the Mississippi River. Meanwhile, in 1855, Henry Wadsworth Longfellow wrote his epic poem "The Song of Hiawatha." The tale of

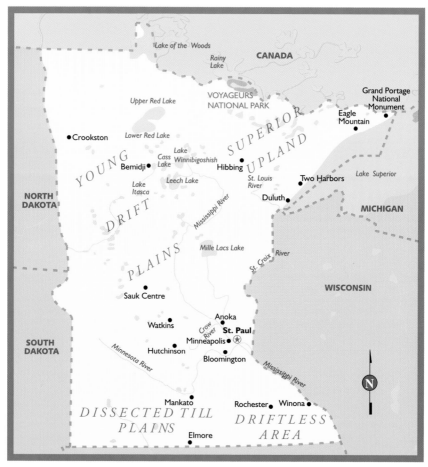

▲ A map of Minnesota.

△ *Over two thousand timber wolves live in the Superior Upland region of Minnesota.*

Hiawatha and his wife, Minnehaha, soon became a crowd pleaser. Minnehaha Falls and Minnehaha Creek are both named after Hiawatha's wife.

▷ Minnesota's Four Regions

Minnesota has four basic land regions: the Superior Upland, the Young Drift Plains, the Dissected Till Plains, and the Driftless Area. The Superior Upland is a region of hard rock. Because of its rocky surface, the glaciers had less effect on this area than on other parts of the state. Minnesota's iron ore deposits are mainly located in this region of high, rugged land. The northeastern tip of the Superior Upland is known as the Arrowhead Country. It is a fitting name for an area shaped like an arrowhead. The

highest point in Minnesota is Eagle Mountain located in Cook County. It is 2,301 feet above sea level.

Much of the Superior Upland region consists of forest wilderness. This region is home to a wide variety of wildlife, including black bears, moose, and bald eagles. More than two thousand timber wolves inhabit this area. This is the largest group of wolves east of the Rocky Mountains. Their numbers are growing due to their status as an endangered species and because of a successful timber wolf recovery program. Some Minnesotans express concern that the expanded numbers of animals create demands that the natural environment cannot fulfill. In some cases, wolves in pursuit of food have killed domestic animals, sheep in particular, but cattle as well.

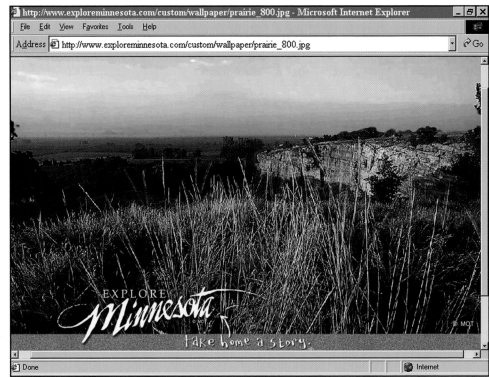

http://www.exploreminnesota.com/custom/wallpaper/prairie_800.jpg - Microsoft Internet Explorer

File　Edit　View　Favorites　Tools　Help

Address http://www.exploreminnesota.com/custom/wallpaper/prairie_800.jpg　Go

Done　Internet

▲ *Prairies can be found in the southwestern part of the state.*

Most of the Young Drift Plains, in central Minnesota, consists of gently-rolling farmlands. The region's fertile soil provides some of the nation's richest farmland. Melting glaciers left behind the fertile topsoil, or drift. In some areas, the glacial action resulted in moraines, which are hilly areas with deposits of stones. Such areas are not suitable for farming.

In the southwestern part of the state is a region known as the Dissected Till Plains. The glaciers in this area left a thick layer of till; a mixture of sand, gravel, and clay. In level areas, soil formed from till makes excellent farmland. The plains in this region are dissected, or cut up, by many streams.

Glaciers never covered the Driftless Area in the southeastern part of the state. The eastern part of the region has deep valleys, while the western part is relatively flat.

▷ Minnesnowta

Some Minnesotans call their state "Minnesnowta."[1] It is a humorous reference to the state's snowy climate. Snow can fall as early as October and as late as May. Northern Minnesota gets about nineteen inches of precipitation per year. The south gets about thirty-two inches. Precipitation includes rain, snow, sleet, etc. Snowfall is actually much higher in the north, even though total annual precipitation is lower. Snowfall in the north is about seventy inches per year, with about twenty inches falling in the south.

In general, the further north you go, the lower the temperatures are, winter or summer. The average January temperature is 2°F in northern Minnesota and 15°F in southern Minnesota. In summer, the average temperature is 68°F in the north and 74°F in the south.

Chapter 3

Economy

Today, Minnesota's economy consists of a broad range of service industries. Businesses related to tourism and various kinds of manufacturing, agriculture, and mining are just a few. However, this was not always true. Early on, Minnesotans mainly depended on natural resources for their livelihoods. The land and what the land provided were everything. During the 1800s, two things drove Minnesota's economy. One was timber; the other was crops. Minnesota's vast forests and fertile farmlands were well known. Then iron-ore mining began in the late 1800s, which also helped to boost the economy.

▶ The Bread and Butter State

One of Minnesota's nicknames, the "Bread and Butter State," dates back to the 1800s. Farming grew rapidly then. Minnesota became known for its dairy products. Likewise, flour mills for grinding wheat into flour sprang up in the state's wheat-growing areas. So much bread was made from wheat flour that Minnesota was often called the Bread Basket. Minneapolis became known as the Mill City. Pillsbury and General Mills are two of Minnesota's most successful companies. They grew out of the original flour mills at the Falls of St. Anthony in Minneapolis. The arrival of the railroads aided the shipping of wheat. Tall grain elevators for storing wheat were built in towns all along the railway lines.

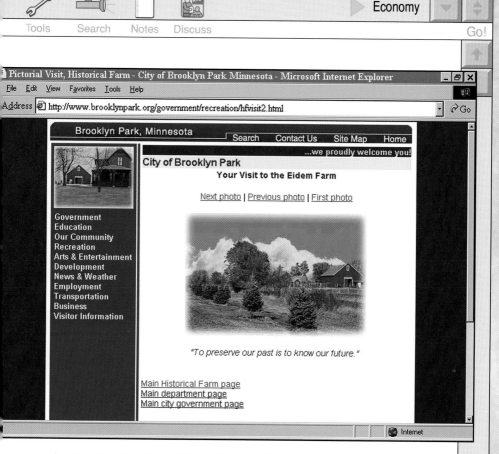

Pictorial Visit, Historical Farm - City of Brooklyn Park Minnesota - Microsoft Internet Explorer

File Edit View Favorites Tools Help

Address http://www.brooklynpark.org/government/recreation/hfvisit2.html   Go

Brooklyn Park, Minnesota   Search   Contact Us   Site Map   Home

...we proudly welcome you!

City of Brooklyn Park
Your Visit to the Eidem Farm

Next photo | Previous photo | First photo

Government
Education
Our Community
Recreation
Arts & Entertainment
Development
News & Weather
Employment
Transportation
Business
Visitor Information

"To preserve our past is to know our future."

Main Historical Farm page
Main department page
Main city government page

Internet

▲ *The Brooklyn Park Historical Farm depicts Minnesotan farm life between the years of 1890 and 1910.*

Today, agriculture accounts for only 2 percent of Minnesota's economy. Only 4 percent of the state's workers are employed in agricultural jobs. Still, farming is important. In fact, Minnesota is one of the leading milk-producing states. Most of the milk is made into butter or cheese. Other important farm products include wheat, wild rice, barley, oats, corn, soybeans, hay, sugar beets, peas, potatoes, and apples. Minnesota is a leading producer of breakfast cereals and canned and frozen vegetables. Minnesota is also an important producer of dairy and beef cattle, hogs, and poultry. Sales of Minnesota's farm products total nearly 7 billion dollars a year.

▶ Logging and Mining

Minnesota's lumber industry began in the 1830s. The state seemed to have an unlimited supply of timber. Lumber camps sprang up all over the north woods. In 1891, lumber mill owner Frederick Weyerhaeuser set up his offices in St. Paul. He had purchased vast tracts of valuable timberland in northern Minnesota. The Weyerhaeuser Company he started in the 1800s is now one of the largest lumber companies in the nation.

Each year 5 million trees are cut down in Minnesota. Many are sold for use as Christmas trees. Others become lumber for construction. Still others are used in the manufacture of paper or products such as materials used

▲ A steam jammer loads logs in the Minnesota National Forest Reserve.

for packaging. For years, lumber companies had cut down trees and left behind a wasteland of stumps where a forest once stood. Today, lumber companies bulldoze the stumps and replant the area. In this way, the forests are renewed, ensuring there will be forests to manage in the future. Indeed, Minnesota now has more trees than it did in 1900!

Northern Minnesota's mining boom began with the discovery of iron ore in 1884 in the Vermilion Range. It was found in the Mesabi Range in 1890. By the 1950s, there was a drop in demand and a drop in the supply of high-grade iron ore. Some mines closed, and the others began producing a low-grade iron ore known as taconite. Today, mining employs only about 2 percent of Minnesota's workforce. Even so, Minnesota is still the nation's largest producer of iron ore.

Minnesota's Seaport

Since Minnesota is located in the center of North America, how is this possible for it to have a seaport? The city of Duluth in northern Minnesota is the farthest-inland ocean port in the United States. It is more than one thousand miles from the Atlantic Ocean. Still, Duluth is North America's busiest freshwater port. Each year, more than twelve hundred oceangoing ships arrive at the docks in Duluth. Many are huge freighters. Most are capable of carrying up to sixty-eight thousand tons of cargo. The ships enter the St. Lawrence River from the Atlantic Ocean. They make their way through the St. Lawrence Seaway. Then they navigate across the Great Lakes. Eventually, the ships arrive at the port of Duluth on the southwestern shore of Lake Superior.

At Duluth, the ships are loaded up with the products from Minnesota's forests, farmlands, and mines. Coal from

Minnehaha Steamboat - Microsoft Internet Explorer

File Edit View Favorites Tools Help

Address http://www.americaslibrary.gov/es/mn/es_mn_steambt_1_e.html

MINNEHAHA.

Done   Internet

▲ The Minnehaha *is one of a fleet of steamships that would take travelers across Lake Minnetonka from one of the Twin Cities to the other. Ridership on these boats declined with the growing popularity of the automobile in the 1920s.*

other states is also shipped out of Duluth. Huge grain elevators store millions of bushels of wheat. It is held there until it is ready for shipping. At Duluth's ore-loading facilities, taconite iron is moved from freight trains onto freighters.

▷ Minnesota Manufacturing

Minnesota companies manufacture a wide variety of products. One of America's best-known manufacturers is 3M. Formerly known as Minnesota Mining and Manufacturing, 3M is located in the Twin Cities. The hundreds of items produced by the company range from Post-it notes to asthma inhalers. Minnesota's electronics companies produce high-tech products of all kinds. Machinery used in the manufacture of computer micro-chips, telecommunications equipment, and medical devices are some examples. Plywood is the leading wood product. Minnesota's lumber is used in the manufacture of everything from baseball bats to toothpicks.

Manufacturing makes up 18 percent of the state's economy. About 14 percent of Minnesota's labor force works in one or another of the state's manufacturing indus-tries. Construction industries account for about 5 percent of the state's economy and employ about 5 percent of the total labor force.

▷ Service Industries

Service industries, including businesses related to tourism, are the largest part of Minnesota's economy. This is about 73 percent of the total. Service industries employ as much as 77 percent of the state's total labor force. Service industries address many needs. These include business, community, and personal services; finance, insurance, and real estate; government services; and communication, transportation, and utilities.

Minneapolis is the center of the state's financial industries. Several major United States banks have their headquarters there. The Twin Cities are also the home of two of the country's major retailing companies. They are SuperValu Stores and the Target Corporation. The Mayo Clinic in Rochester is one of the largest medical centers in the world. Dr. William Mayo and his sons, William and

▲ *Minneapolis is essential to Minnesota's economy, because it houses the state's financial district. Service industries such as finance make up approximately 73 percent of the state's commerce.*

Charles, founded the Mayo Clinic in 1889. Greyhound Bus Lines began as a local bus service in Hibbing in 1914, later moving its headquarters to Duluth. Today it is the nation's largest bus system.

Government

On May 11, 1858, the Minnesota Territory entered the Union as the thirty-second state. In planning for statehood, a territorial convention had drawn up the Minnesota Constitution in July of the previous year. In October 1857, the territorial legislature adopted the new state constitution.

▶ The Structure of Minnesota's Government

The Minnesota Constitution outlines the structure of the state's government. It spells out the powers of the different branches of the government. It also describes the rights

△ St. Paul is Minnesota's state capital. Visitors may take guided tours of the state capitol building (shown here).

and responsibilities of Minnesota's citizens and their elected officials.

Minnesota's state government is based on a separation of powers, like the federal government and the governments of the other states. The Minnesota Constitution divides the state government into three branches: the executive, the legislative, and the judicial. The executive branch carries out the laws; the legislative branch creates the laws; and the judicial branch interprets the laws.

Minnesota's voters elect the governor, the head of the executive branch, to a four-year term of office. There is no limit to the number of times the governor can be reelected. The other key elected officials of the executive branch include the lieutenant governor, secretary of state, attorney general, treasurer, and auditor. They serve four-year terms. The governor appoints the heads of most state departments, boards, and commissions. These officials serve terms ranging from two to six years.

The legislative branch of Minnesota's state government consists of a state senate and a house of representatives. Most senators serve a four-year term in office, with one exception—senators elected in years divisible by ten serve two-year terms. The legislators' main job is to propose new laws. The governor can veto legislation and appropriation bills drawn up by the state legislature. The legislature, however, can override the veto with a two-thirds vote of the lawmakers in each house.

The judicial branch of Minnesota's government consists of the state supreme court and a district court that is divided into ten judicial districts. The chief justice and six associate justices of the state supreme court are elected to six-year terms. Minnesota's judicial district judges also serve six-year terms. The district court handles criminal and civil cases. In 1982, an amendment to Minnesota's Constitution established a court of appeals. Judges of the court of appeals are elected to six-year terms.

▷ Minnesota's Progressive Political Leaders

Hubert H. Humphrey (1911–78), one of Minnesota's most famous politicians. He once said, "that the moral test of government is how that government treats those who are in the dawn of life, the children; those who are in the twilight of life, the elderly; and those who are in the shadows of life, the sick, the needy, and the handicapped."[1] Humphrey was describing his own progressive approach to

▲ Hubert Horatio Humphrey was a progressive political leader. Upon his death in 1978, President Jimmy Carter eulogized Humphrey by saying, "From time to time, our nation is blessed by the presence of men and women who bear the mark of greatness, who help us see a better vision of what we can become. Hubert Humphrey was such a man."

political leadership. As mayor of Minneapolis, he became the first American mayor to put through a law that guaranteed fair employment for minorities. Later, as a U.S. senator from Minnesota, he fought for passage of the 1964 Civil Rights Act and introduced a bill to establish the Peace Corps. Humphrey served in the U.S. Senate for twenty-three years. He was vice president of the United States from 1965 to 1969, serving under President Lyndon B. Johnson.

Eugene McCarthy was born in Watkins, Minnesota, in 1916. He served Minnesota in the U.S. House of Representatives and in the U.S. Senate. An outspoken critic of U.S. involvement in the Vietnam War, McCarthy ran unsuccessfully for president in 1968.

Walter Mondale was born in Elmore, Minnesota, in 1928. Mondale served as a U.S. senator from Minnesota for twelve years. He later served as vice president of the United States from 1977 to 1981, under President Jimmy Carter. He made an unsuccessful run for the presidency in 1984.

Harold Stassen (1907–2001) served as governor of Minnesota from 1939 to 1943. He was only thirty-one years old when he became governor, the youngest person ever elected to that office in the United States. In 1945, Stassen helped set up the United Nations. He opposed the testing of nuclear weapons and supported giving financial aid to poor countries.

In 1998, Jesse Ventura became the nation's first Reform Party candidate elected governor. He was born James George Janos in Minneapolis in 1951. Ventura is a former professional wrestler and Navy SEAL. He is outspoken and direct in his approach to political issues.

History

The first Minnesotans were descendants of hunters who had migrated from Asia to North America. During the last Ice Age, much of North America was buried under thick sheets of ice. A land bridge extended from Asia to North America across what is now the Bering Strait. About forty thousand years ago, hunters known as nomads began

▲ The Dakota tribes living on the plains of Minnesota were nomadic. Dakota hunters moved with the buffalo herds because buffalo were their main food source.

migrating across the land bridge from Siberia (in Asia) to Alaska (in North America). Nomads have no permanent homes. Instead, they follow herds of wild animals as they search for food and water. By around twelve thousand years ago, various groups of nomadic hunters had spread southward and eastward throughout the Americas. The first groups entered what is now Minnesota.

American Indians of Minnesota

The first inhabitants of Minnesota, known as Paleo-Indians, are ancestors of today's American Indians. Scientists have discovered broken spear points and other stone objects along the shores of Lake of the Woods, on Minnesota's northern border. They believe the artifacts to be about twelve thousand years old. For several thousand years, the Paleo-Indians, sometimes called "Big Game" people, hunted large animals such as mammoths and mastodons for food and clothing.

Descendants of the Paleo-Indians continued to live a nomadic lifestyle. Eventually these early Minnesotans learned how to make tools and weapons out of copper. This metal was common throughout the region. The Copper Culture existed in Minnesota from about 5000 B.C. to 1000 B.C. Petroglyphs, pictures carved on rock faces and on the sides of cliffs, date from this period. The Jeffers Petroglyphs in southwestern Minnesota are believed to be about five thousand years old.

After 1000 B.C., groups of American Indians belonging to the Northeast Woodland Culture thrived in Minnesota. They hunted deer, elk, and moose in the forests. In the area's many lakes and streams, they fished for sturgeon, pike, and whitefish. They also gathered berries and wild rice. By the A.D. 1600s, there were two main groups of

American Indians in Minnesota: the Dakota and the Chippewa. The Dakota included various clans throughout central, northern, and western Minnesota. The Dakota who lived in the woods built dome-shaped, birch-bark homes called wigwams. Those on the prairies followed the herds of buffalo. They rode horses and hunted the buffalo with bows and arrows. They lived in teepees that were easy to move from one place to another. The Chippewa, called Ojibwe in Canada, lived in permanent villages along the shores of Lake Superior.

The Dakota and Chippewa became bitter enemies. Whenever the Chippewa ventured inland, they fought

http://collections.mnhs.org/visualresources/image.cfm?imageid=160272&RecCount=55 - Microsoft Intern...

File   Edit   View   Favorites   Tools   Help

Address http://collections.mnhs.org/visualresources/image.cfm?imageid=160272&RecCount=55   Go

Done   Internet

By 1857, American Indian tribes, such as the Dakota and Chippewa, were isolated on small reservations while over fifty thousand white settlers inhabited the rest of Minnesota.

over hunting grounds with the Dakota. Indeed, the Chippewa called the Dakota *Nadouessioux*, meaning "little snakes." The first white men called the Dakota "Sioux." This was a shortened form of Nadouessioux. The people of the Sioux Nation prefer to be called by their individual tribal names, for example, Dakota and Lakota, to name just two.[1]

French Explorers and Fur Traders

Pierre Esprit Radisson and Médard Chouart des Groseilliers arrived at what is now Two Harbors, Minnesota, in 1660. The two French fur traders were the first known white men to set foot in the area. They paddled their birch-bark canoe across the waterways of Minnesota's wilderness. In search of furs, they explored much of the forests of what is now the northern part of the state. The two explorers traded with the Chippewa. Cloth, cooking utensils, whiskey, and guns were exchanged for furs.

Other Frenchmen followed. Daniel Greysolon Duluth arrived in Minnesota in 1679. He landed on the shore of Lake Superior. After exploring the area, he claimed the region for France. One of Duluth's outposts later grew to become the city of Duluth.

In 1680, a Belgian missionary, named Father Louis Hennepin, and two companions explored the upper Mississippi River area. They were the first white men to visit the site of present-day Minneapolis. There they discovered and named the Falls of St. Anthony. The Dakota captured Hennepin along with his companions. The three men were later rescued by Duluth.

In the following years, more Frenchmen arrived to trade with the Indians. For a time, there was peace between the Chippewa and the Dakota. Both tribes cooperated with each other in delivering furs to the French. However, in 1736, the Dakota killed twenty Frenchmen over a trade dispute. The Chippewa rushed to support the French. Peace ceased between the two tribes. For the next one hundred years, the Chippewa and the Dakota would continue to fight.

Minnesota Becomes a U.S. Territory

The area that is now Minnesota would change hands several times before finally becoming a territory of the United States. During the years 1762 to 1812, Spain, France, and Britain would each claim and reclaim lands in this region.

History of Minnesota - Microsoft Internet Explorer

File   Edit   View   Favorites   Tools   Help

Address http://emuseum.mnsu.edu/history/mnstatehistory/   Go

Sod House - Lac qui Parle County, Minnesota

Menu activated   Internet

△ *Due to the lack of lumber on the prairies of Minnesota, many pioneers were forced to build their houses of sod.*

In 1805, U.S. President Thomas Jefferson sent Lieutenant Zebulon M. Pike to explore the lands acquired in the Louisiana Purchase of 1803. Pike incorrectly identified the Mississippi's source as Upper Red Cedar Lake. Today, Upper Red Cedar Lake is known as Cass Lake. It was not until 1832 that Henry Rowe Schoolcraft discovered the river's true source, Lake Itasca. He created the name "Itasca," from the Latin words *veritas*, meaning "truth," and *caput*, meaning "head."

In 1820, the U.S. Army began building a fort at the junction of the Mississippi and Minnesota rivers, just south of the present site of the Twin Cities. The fort, named Fort Snelling, was completed in 1825. It stood on a bluff overlooking the rivers. To attract settlers, the army built a sawmill and a flour mill. Settlers began arriving in the area during the early 1820s. Most of them came by steamboat up the Mississippi from St. Louis and other towns to the south. The first steamboat arrived at Fort Snelling in 1823. The settlers believed the presence of soldiers would protect them from the fighting between the Chippewa and Dakota.

As more and more settlers arrived in Minnesota, it was only a matter of time before the American Indians began to resent them. The settlers had not come to trade with the native people. Instead, they cut down trees and planted crops, driving wild game farther away. The United States government pressured the American Indians into selling their lands. The native tribes signed treaties giving up more and more of their land. The government often did not honor the terms of the treaties.

By 1849, there were almost five thousand white settlers in Minnesota. That year, U.S. President Zachary Taylor created the Minnesota Territory. To encourage settlement, the federal government offered to sell land in Minnesota for $1.25 an acre. By 1857, most of the American Indians' former lands belonged to white settlers. The Dakota lived on a small reservation along the Minnesota River. The Chippewa lived on a few small pieces of land in northern Minnesota. Meanwhile, more than fifty thousand pioneers had settled in Minnesota. There were few trees available on the prairie. Therefore, the settlers had to build houses out of sod—hardened dirt held together by grass. Lumber companies in Minnesota's northern forests prospered as the demand for building materials grew.

▲ The pink and white lady slipper is Minnesota's state flower. It is the rarest wildflower in the state, and it is illegal to pick. With a lifespan of fifty years, the lady slipper takes four to sixteen years just to yield its first bloom.

▷ Statehood Leads to Rapid Growth

Minnesota became the thirty-second state in the Union on May 11, 1858. By this time, its population had grown to about 150,000.

The Civil War period (1861–65), was a tragic time for many Minnesotans. The Santee Sioux, a branch of the Dakota tribe, decided to make war on the settlers. The Santee's crops had failed because of a drought. In addition, the government refused to give the Santee the money and supplies that had been promised to them. The tribal leader, Chief Little Crow, advised against war. Still, the younger leaders were eager to fight. Little Crow said, "You are fools. You will die like the rabbits when the hungry wolves hunt them in the hard moon [winter]. [Little Crow] is not a coward. [I] will die with you."[2]

The American Indians attacked frontier towns and settlers' homes on the prairie. Close to five hundred settlers were killed. Many others fled. The Santee Sioux were finally defeated when federal troops reinforced Minnesota's militiamen. About sixty warriors were killed in the fighting. On December 26, 1862, thirty-eight Santee were hanged. Little Crow had escaped. However, in July 1863, while picking berries near Hutchinson, Minnesota, Little Crow was fatally shot by a soldier.

Also in 1862, President Abraham Lincoln signed the Homestead Act. This new law guaranteed the arrival of huge numbers of new settlers. According to the Homestead Act, settlers going west would be given 160 acres of free land to farm. In the coming years, Minnesota's population would soar.

After the Civil War ended in 1865, railroads were built across Minnesota. The war had halted work on some; others were entirely new. One of Minnesota's nicknames is the "Gopher State." The name came from the "Gopher Cartoon," an 1857 political cartoon about railroads. At the time, Minnesota lawmakers wanted to issue bonds to help pay for the building of railroad tracks. Those who opposed the bonds published the cartoon. It showed ten men weighed down by heavy bags full of bribery money. On their backs was a train on railroad tracks. The train was pulled by nine gophers.

By the 1870s, more than one hundred trains pulled into the busy St. Paul Union Depot each day. Many new immigrants arrived on each train. The state's population grew from 430,000 in 1870 to about 1.2 million in 1890. Farming, especially wheat farming, spread rapidly.

▲ Economic recovery after World War II, the birth of the Baby Boom generation, and an increase in automobile ownership in the 1950s and 1960s caused an even greater shift in population from rural areas to urban cities such as Minneapolis (shown here).

Minnesota's economy, based on logging, farming, and then iron-ore mining, grew vigorously.

▷ Building a Brighter Future

During the 1890s and early 1900s, many of Minnesota's farmers joined farm cooperatives. They were looking for a more economical way to provide important services. This included such things as the transportation and storage of their products, as well as financial services. Farming was such an important part of the state's economy that it had an effect on Minnesota's politics. During the 1920s, the Farmer-Labor Party represented the interests of Minnesota's farmers. In 1931, Floyd B. Olson became the first Farmer-Labor governor. In 1944, the Farmer-Labor Party joined the Democratic Party. The new combined party was called the Democratic-Farmer-Labor Party.

By 1950, more Minnesotans lived in the state's cities than in the rural areas. Manufacturing companies made more money than farms. Minneapolis had become a thriving industrial center. As early as 1882, the city sold electricity generated from rushing water. Minneapolis, thanks to the Falls of St. Anthony, was the first place in the United States to generate hydroelectric power. In the mid-1900s, new manufacturing industries were developing in all of the state's urban areas. Many people moved to the cities to take advantage of job opportunities.

Today, Minnesota has a thriving and diverse economy. People are still drawn to the Twin Cities because of the cultural attractions as well as the job opportunities that are there. Minnesotans enjoy the natural beauty and recreational possibilities of their state's many lakes and the vast wilderness areas of the northern forests. Minnesotans have found ways to protect their state's environment from the

▲ *Air quality measured in the Twin Cities was consistently better than the national average during the 1990s.*

harmful effects of pollution. Taconite-mining companies no longer discharge waste into Lake Superior. Other industries, encouraged by the state government, make an effort to control pollution. Minnesotans are proud that, in 2000, Morgan Quitno Press ranked Minnesota as the "most livable" state.

Minnesota Facts

1. "All About Minnesota," *North Star: Minnesota Government Information and Services*, March 4, 2001, <http://www.state.mn.us/> (November 3, 2002).

Chapter 1. The State of Minnesota

1. Arlene Hirschfelder and Martha Kriepe de Montaño, *The Native American Almanac: A Portrait of Native America Today* (New York: Prentice Hall, 1993), p. 87.

2. Mark Lightbody, *Great Lakes* (Hawthorn, Victoria, Australia: Lonely Planet Publications, 2000), p. 482.

3. "All About Minnesota," *North Star: Minnesota Government Information and Services*, April 20, 2001, <http://www.state.mn.us/> (November 3, 2002).

4. "Minnesota Historic Sites: Charles A. Lindbergh Historic Site," *Minnesota Historical Society*, n.d., <http://www.mnhs.org/places/sites/lh/index.html> (October 22, 2002).

Chapter 2. Land and Climate

1. Mark Lightbody, *Great Lakes* (Hawthorn, Victoria, Australia: Lonely Planet Publications, 2000), p. 482.

Chapter 4. Government

1. Hubert H. Humphrey, as quoted by Brainymedia, "Quote: Hubert H. Humphrey," *BrainyQuote*, 2003, <http://www.brainyquote.com/quotes/quotes/h/q/31146.html> (January 17, 2003).

Chapter 5. History

1. "The Great Sioux Nation," *The Rosebud Sioux Homepage*, n.d., <http://www.tradecorridor.com/rosebud/nation.htm> (October 22, 2002).

2. Chief Little Crow, as quoted by Douglas O. Linder, "Little Crow," *Famous Trials Homepage*, 1999, <http://www.law.umkc.edu/faculty/projects/ftrials/dakota/LittleCrow.html> (January 13, 2003).

Capstone Press Staff. *Minnesota*. Minnetonka, Minn.: Capstone Press, Inc., 1997.

Fradin, Dennis Brindell, and Judith Bloom Fradin. *Minnesota*. Chicago: Children's Press, 1994.

Gilman, Rhoda R. *The Story of Minnesota's Past*. St. Paul: Minnesota Historical Society Press, 1991.

Hintz, Martin. *Minnesota*. Danbury, Conn.: Children's Press, 2000.

Kallen, Stuart A. *Minnesota*. Farmington Hills, Mich.: Gale Group, 2001.

Murphy, Nora, and Mary Murphy-Gnatz. *Meet African Americans in Minnesota: Telling Our Own Stories*. Saint Paul, Minn.: Minnesota Historical Society Press, 2000.

Porter, A. P. *Minnesota*. Minneapolis: Lerner Publications Co., 2002.

———. *Minnesota: Hello U.S.A.* Minneapolis: Lerner Publishing Group, 1996.

Purslow, Neil. *A Guide to Minnesota*. Mankato, Minn.: Weigl Publishers, Inc., 2002.

Thompson, Kathleen. *Minnesota*. Austin, Tex.: Raintree Steck-Vaughn Publishers, 1996.

Index